T0151979

3 SUMMERS

Lisa Robertson

art by Hadley
Maxwell

Coach House Books,
Toronto

2016

first edition

 Canada Council   Conseil des Arts      ONTARIO ARTS COUNCIL   Canadä
for the Arts   du Canada   CONSEIL DES ARTS DE L'ONTARIO
                                                           an Ontario government agency
                                                           un organisme du gouvernement de l'Ontario

Published with the generous assistance of the Canada Council for
the Arts and the Ontario Arts Council. Coach House Books also
acknowledges the support of the Government of Canada through
the Canada Book Fund and the Government of Ontario through the
Ontario Book Fund.

LIBRARY AND ARCHIVES CANADA CATALOGUING IN PUBLICATION

Robertson, Lisa, 1961-, author
    3 summers / Lisa Robertson.

ISBN 978-1-55245-330-8

    I. Title. II. Title: Three summers.

PS8585.O3217A13 2016   C811'.54   C2016-904400-9

3 Summers is available as an ebook: ISBN 978 1 77056 480 0 (EPUB),
ISBN 978 1 77056 481 7 (PDF), ISBN 978 1 77056 482 4 (MOBI)

a minimum of sensible time

a minimum of thinkable time

a time smaller than the minimum

a time smaller than the minimum of thinkable time

a minimum of continuous thinkable time

a time smaller than the minimum of sensible time

a minimum of continuous sensible time

Contents

The Seams

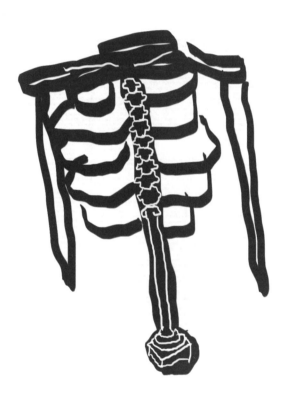

4:16 in the afternoon in the summer of my 52nd year
I'm lying on the bed in the heat wondering about geometry
as the deafening, uninterrupted volume of desire
bellows, roars mournfully, laments
like a starling that has flown into glass.
These are two things that I want to remember permanently:
the dog straining diagonally after the hare at dusk last night
and the glittering disco sky.
I am no longer afraid of being misunderstood when I state
the old men's docile gadgetry –
I don't buy it.
What suits me better is to stargaze or to lie in stylish baths.
Now it's time to return to the sex of my thinking.
How long do I get?
A fly moves across the pages of an open book
(the pages are quivering)
I want stimulants, relaxants, hallucinogens
– I'm not good at order.

The men who tremble a little bit
while speaking about passivity –
they're all right. I could compare them
to a song:

        You should live twice in time
        Were I contingent
        Upon your heart, your spleen
        Or embody the spate

Then collapse
Of love, the living creature.

To add gravitas
I am alone, transcribing
If you can never be mine
I'll get some Swinburne.

There is the sense of women
As impairment's ability
That's how it falls
Perilous, unoptional
It's difficult to sing.

Using Ovid maybe
You'd lay your tongue across my art
Loved face
The poem is a hormone.

I have no idea what song means
That polishes the heart.

We press out these voices from the inmost parts
to be able to start.
Sometimes desire awakens the ears of a whole crowd
with copious particularity
with the urgent motions of membranes
with the mystic dialectic of toxins and hormones
(more hormones, less toxins; less hormones, more

toxins; movement between toxins and
hormones and also their confusion
for hormones can act as toxins and
toxins can act as hormones) so that
the fear of death falls away for a minute.
Venus breaks a dew at the borders of everything.
Right now when I think of her
I have no problem with the feminine pronoun.
I'm stupid against its animate insult, me
with my scaly feet, my rubbed thorax
my vibrating wings, my periodic
radiation, my repetitive chant and cunt

A fly moves across the pages of an open book
(the wind riffles the pages slightly)
I think of girls saying *I* in novels
people saying *we* in plazas and restaurants
students and cops –

People's mouths are brutal portable things.
The pronoun is gratuitous expenditure
as necessity.
I was a daughter in blouses
a sucker in stairwells
I was the only human to ever feel desire
for the fly moving across the open book
for the shimmer of gnats above a frugal terrace
I'm stupid against flowers, quotas
I'm stupid against tables

all my cells bust
I got a little shipwreck, a frugal little ship
shipwrecked
on a decorated terrace
– it's hard not to play this as testimony –
I was a sucker in blouses, I was the only human
to ever say *we*, I sat at frugal tables and
I undertook the ceremony of brutality
or pronouns. I knelt I bust
a testimony I was a shimmer
of gnats at noon I was living in a hut
as a form of protest and it didn't matter I lied
and I held it together and the light
was for my body and the fly
was a shipwreck. To thee I went
but I didn't. I shelter my lesion.

Some are masters of desire, all deferral
and expletives, using the word triumphant
while they lounge in their marriages.
To choose, to think, to mean, to gather
to eagerly pursue the shimmer that can't cohere
above the table, to occupy the silent terrace
as the flowers just pour upwards
to be organized towards sugar
why not

But then we would become enemies.
Innovation is not a quality –

I want you to really mean it.
Truth is, everything that isn't poetry bores me
and within the problem of lamentation
is my perennial resistance-sensation.
I'm telling you things you already know
to keep myself intact.
There is no everyday life.
That was a bribe from the masters.
I've taken down the curtains so I can watch the foliage move.
To be accurate, to be objective
my idea of myself relates to landscape's
unimagined achievement.
An event I never sought
will shift through the frail silence
as I sit in a chair not moving.
We have loved nothing, brutally.
The DNA of loss moves through leaves –
some hidden occident of vibration
played on a disintegrating cassette tape
to the tune of you are the tenderness of strangers
half-sleeping on a train.

Gods still move by river
the flat warehouses
are country-like
and I wonder about silt and trees and chemicals
as boats are loaded.
What if the body does not signify?
Its wee lost cluster

starts to fade
the skin opening to the moisture of the season
its immunity is landscape
(here by landscape I mean political economy)

To have a bath, to write in bed in a hotel
so obvious and so easy
an entire day till the light starts to fade
to arrive at the long duration of an instability.
How to walk with this till the end
speak its tongue like a guest
at the discontinuous table
my hands shake
lilacs are everywhere

This fundamental torsion
so thoroughly unskirtable
there will never again be sex in 1983 and
I don't mind really.
Must I fear formlessness?
If it weren't for song I'd be free
as body organs cast in metals
– divinatory objects –
to decorate time
I like to spit from moving trains.

So much can be passed over
in avoidance of the rupture
the driver of the team of 6 horses ploughing

is a woman, cotton sleeves
rolled to elbow, hands to straining
harness – skinny, capable –
my kinship with this woman
her 6 huge horses and the surge
of their vitality running through leather into my body
we who have no memories at all
mount the pulsing tree in evening
every desire emits
a throw of dice
I start a school called how can I live.

In my school called how can I live
in my theory of appearing
I lay out my costume.
We don't belong to culture. We're sunsets.
We simplify thought
until it resembles
stripes.
Our skin itches.
I beg you – show me something unknowable.
I don't believe in this possibility of knowing.
Stop hiding from life! we say to ourselves.
As for the image
how will it start?
The flipped-over buses
the strange stuff suspended in the air
while they copulate they turn their heads
towards the east.

Tell me now about shame and isolation
the shame that has not even
a vocabulary
– it just distracts us from our purpose.
Sometimes I see things and I know right away
like looking someone in the eye.
The great health is unknown gratuitous expenditure towards
the material ideal.
It is not a metaphor.
From now on, everything will be called The Middle, everything
will be called The Seam, everything will be called Toxins,
everything will be called The Great Health.
Everything will be a hormone.

TOXINS

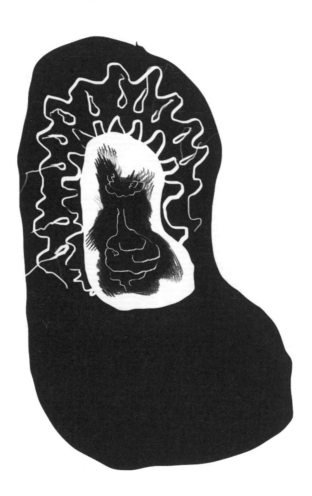

Go now. Recite your poem to your aunt.

I threw myself to the ground.

Where were you in the night?

In a school among the pines.

What was the meaning of the dream?

A rough clay bottle. A carved wooden saltbox with a swivel lid.

A tin travelling trunk painted green.

What would feel like home?

What would a school feel like?

I haven't yet been satisfied.

Let's organize a pageant.

Many boys, dressed as nymphs, each carrying an olive branch.

What do you see?

I'm not looking out the window.

Everything is half finished.

Where is my seagull?

There.

Walking between the field and the last houses at 10 p.m.
holding the lilacs aloft like a torch
its vital sense of pause
everything will be hesitation
the acts of transposition
muscular, tactile, olfactory
where the image itself senses.

The pinky moon was swishing all
quivering-flanked
heaves, vomits, sniffs her
vomit, looks to the horizon, sniffs the
air, standing still, looking, ears erect – She
was fluttering, falling, fundamentally
somatic, fanning like hearts, a distant
name in an exotic and privileged
setting – Miuccia Prada for
instance – pulsing upwardly post-
metaphysical and if I sit at
my desk in my big coat it's because words
are cold.

Now, the glorious suture or the
philosophy of the tree. The tree doesn't 'have'
'a body.' This means that when it comes to
the need for changing, the tree just waits. It
takes all my art to live beside a tree
with uncaused devotion and the
abandonment of determinism and
I am sad.

When I learned grief, its arms changed
into the forelegs of an animal
and bark climbed upwards to sheath its hips
I also longed to be under
that bark, I longed for my own hoofs. Then
I threw off my green coat and I clenched my hands
and I throve
and thriving shamed me.

Which brings about a beautiful idea –
in history there is always someone
and there is what someone has made:
a polder
of half-scale kitchen chairs and used file folders
and research as pleasure. This slight revolt
distributes itself frothlike over
a social surface, and it is large enough
to hold everything. It is the liberation
of matter. What does that look like? I want
to know too, but I think it's not
optical.

I dream of running to escape into the cornfield.
Inside the cornfield I find tiny battered civilizations.
They give me something to do.

How does it work?
Listening to Tom Jones on vinyl and reading Carlyle?
Why didn't I say emotion?
Why did I say documents?
I used the language of a baroque politics.
That was a real lie.

Waking up in cabins in 1979
is the polder of happiness like that?
the long slash of pure gold
opening up behind the utility shed
shabby and powerless
the low lichen
the deep fog –
How does it work?

That time we called our theory Toxins
we became adepts of its excellence.
We thought our city would be a place
but it is a leak
and I will feel shame
mortal shame that I am not a tree.
How can I make time out of toxins?

We were eating these huge boiled flowers.
We were always running away from our bodies and then we weren't.
Mostly my sex was blind and stupid and this was a way to live.
The mystic who's in love with time
eats an idealized meal.

Or quite indifferent
rhyme returns
as brutal as the impersonal damp
the non-human body of the damp
feeding the stove of god.

Health is unlegislated
it unfurls raw on the table
the extent to which its meaning does not exist ripens
a thousand years pass.

The movement, just outside perception
traverses limbs, skin, organs, hair
as if it were the purpose of this sentiment not to be expressed.
Its scale is unknown but pervasive.

The one that goes cack-cack-cack
the one that whinnies like a colt at the back of the field
perhaps they have plundered the mediocrity of capital
to parody it as sensation.

The great elaborate theme
crumples slowly, heavily, elaborately
nudging forward against the picture plane
like a non-supernatural experience that transfigures things
by way of fit, drape, weight, mode of fastening
unstoppable reverie and overdetermination.
Sometimes one is
an elephant
leaving physics behind
for cosmology
sometimes the body is quiet
in its great effort to avoid equilibrium.

On Form

for Jane Ellison

You could say that form is learning

you can see form take shape

at the coronal suture's first arcade

it's explaining it's appearing

unestranged from enormity's

prick of a spiny plant like a rose

experimenting it's bursting and

usually it's repeating why is form

a dog as a horse as a deer as a

fish and a bramble a grater rapacious

the second cervical vertebra is

repeating is a question we can

ask with our bodies and what is

a tooth coccyx is the beak of an ancient

dove below the sacrum the tip of

the sacrum places in the person a

sensation of slow form repeating it

doesn't require its own skin to repeat

fox a foxtail a lizard as psoas

a small flask of modern oil at the throat

the repeat carries between bodies

what's made in this space are theories

and thymus a rising of beneficial

smoke as thorax as guitar the hairs

exact and between bodies form's

not ever without a stupendous body

so the repetition is never exact

this is why form is always learning

as it moves across surfaces as

on the cleft above the lips to be

repetition is never exact this is why

form is learning or becoming or how

as it moves across timely surfaces

including the intricately folded surfaces

sucked when kissing sometimes the lower

lip has a crease like a waking girl in

the real territory of the conceptual

the liver is a crown and it is a vessel

it constitutes our life form is folding

the full part is a vase the nostril is

cartilage connecting mineral salts

the root of the belly the palate a

celestial dome a vault a sky a

nylon-like connecting dissolving

palace the tongue is a stitch a root a

complex tissue of crystalline constituents

as freefloating folds motivating

intestines as a nest the bowel is

blind the rectum founds it all the anus

is a ring a door a precipice the

nervous system orients vast complexities

to make them even less efficient we're

trying to solve efficiency luckily

the sphincter's a crow the liver's a

table a summit a choir a door the

tracheal artery is a country

flute the lungs are apples each part of a

heart is named differently but

it seems to be prettily resisting

generally heart is a vase with little

ears the spinal column is a canal

out towards the periphery and also

of marrow the thorax is also a

tortoise and a stall the ribs are fronds and

these are found in the same lake

they are spades the greater ribs are boats they

are maritime together the ribs form

a kind of anywhere-ness and anyone-ness

the teeth of a comb which is not only

a grooming implement but a tool for

their role as relations in a behaviour

as weavers the rib cage thus their loom the

shoulder blades are plates and they make writing

pads or little desks these desks are winged

when our hands feel empty they are not empty

the clavicles are keys and they close and

open the gate between the throat and

sweetly there is a suture there

touch is a really unstable compound

metaphor but it does have a head the

radius is a tailor or drumstick

a brooch and historically a hinge

the hand is a rustic cheeseplate the

same for the feet the fingers are a phalanx

of snakes or of fishes the skin is treebark

in this place the voice is touching us

it comes down to a physiological

work this is a representational

problem something like memory

work this is a transformational work

about the domestic nature economy

sufficient yet imperceptible

it is medicinal the cheeks are melons

are bowls or concepts or clods the stomach

is a mouth nostrils are the lairs of little

animals or fish a choirmaster names them

indistinguishable from anarchy

every cell's means of turning every

thing into transcendent operatic

the heart as well as the liver we can

compare the liver to a city or

a mansion and the intestines are the

market gardens surrounding it the veins

are roads leading up to the city gates

no proper limit no verbal chain continually altering

the cardiac veins are wee snakes the ear's

continually altering internal conditions

a measuring cup and a conch

they are among the kitchen utensils

between our nerve endings and our motor units

like the female sex that thrives behind

the earlobe there is a bony poppy

fucking wildly at the edge of capital

this experience can constitute a break

in sincerity density and scale

the helix of the ear is a bracelet

the ear is also a hive it produces

wax which is a humour it is the nest

of a swallow as well the eye sockets

are basins for washing grain the eye is

carnival artifice intrigue

wandering's root the eyeball like a sun

like a cheek like a breast the white of the

eye is a river pebble the glance is

a throw of stones the iris is a rain

on this conceptual meta-membrane

ah luxuriant nomad pubis

the eyelid is skirt the eyelashes are

the outer surface of the mind

album berry or nymph pip barleycorn hill

or sparrows completely and ardently

send us action thriving foray touch

this suture right now

On Physical Real Being and What Happens Next

I feel ambivalent about adoring
The sex of Mars
Like America it basks
Exempt from dolorous stuff
The imperium's fucked up
How can we kiss and think?

I make a model
with folded paper
of the exigent season called Spring
Venus emerges
her sea-scarf's swirling –

go Venus go vernal go turning go
darling by folding sky by buoyant kiss

by plenty (I lie in bed and read Marx)
by secret breezes twisting, contriving

by boulevards by cattle by springle
a springald a springet rise agile from

water, go down modern to the natal
turn by rapacious meetings by luminous

flowers – take with you the eagerness of
my submission to the proliferate

material discipline also
called speech as the political feeling

lusts for public light by engorged
rivers by populated foliage

by veering campus the cry of desire
a morning blackbird in the city entirely

secular and generative and I
can't curtail my life.

I want a pause in vocation. Venus
chatoyant in the formal dream
please tranquilize efficient Mars and his
efficient interests. Do it like this:

The man's neck's flung back
his man-shawl's agitated
he has the soul of a mortal horse
and his saliva's communal
flung supine beneath
the concept of a goddess
who unclasps the depth of his torso
with her skilled goddess mouth
(consciousness is their consciousness)
now recite sap and flower juice to the nation
(a lemon falls to pavement outside their window)
Do it like this.

Cognition in the room
felt like sensuous human activity
real sensuous activity as such
and natality's ornate
quiescence tied to fear's
superb circumference at
home in the dominant expressive
housekeeping of the street
a composition is set in motion.
Unmotivated by any bodily movement
Marx finds in Lucretius the defiant probability.

The I-speaker
on her silken rupture
spills into history.

Of the life of Lucretius one can say that we know practically nothing.

Our certain knowledge of the life of T. Lucretius Carus can be stated in a sentence.

Nothing is known of his life.

Of Lucretius's life, remarkably little is known.

Apart from this poem, Lucretius is scarcely more than a name.

Very little is known of the poet's life.

We know virtually nothing.

No exact deduction is possible from the mention of his name by two contemporaries.

It is doubtful both when T. Lucretius Carus was born and when he died.

These are the sole circumstances recorded of his life, nor is anything whatever known about his family.

There is no direct evidence in regard to the birthplace of Lucretius.

The life of Lucretius has been all but forgotten.

Sometimes I need a record
Knowing it doesn't matter
And sometimes I need
A flower machine.

Here is Marx's big dilemma, the reason he goes to Lucretius:
practice arises from conditions
yet these are the conditions we must change.
With a cloth on her upraised right hand
Venus stands on a shell, hair windblown, torso twisted to dance
    posture, more fluttering cloth draped over her arm.
As Lucretius writes, Rome is torn by civil strife.
Something of the murky tumult of his times shadows his verses.
In his boyhood began the civil wars.
The Goddess is stepping out of a shell in the midst of the sea.
The stress and turmoil of his times stand in the background.
Lucretius is a man of peace.
He keeps much aloof.
On the left are two winds flying across the waves and propelling
    the Goddess towards land. Life-sized.
The text may have become politically disreputable.

The transitory movements of hair and garments won't dissolve
    into tradition.
Sounds of every sort are surging through the air
Myrtle Poppy Apple Sparrow
the fortuities of a name are being pushed
in the philosophy tradition
indigent, uninvented, unconvertible twisting
Too frail!
She is prosodic.
Her theme has always aroused controversy.

According to St. Jerome (c. 340–420 CE), Lucretius in a fit of insanity took his own life.

But what of the other elements in Jerome – the love-philtre, the madness, the lucid intervals of poetic activity, and the suicide, all of which Tennyson has made so famous?

They say he was insane, at times an honorable epithet. He may have committed suicide.

A legend, which goes back to Scaliger, followed by Tennyson for poetic reasons in his Lucretius, that his wife killed him by a love-potion, has nothing to support it, and we do not even know that he had a wife.

There is a similar doubt as to his suicide.

It is doubtful what truth, if any, lies behind the traditional story (immortalized by Tennyson) that he died by his own hand after being driven mad by a love-philtre.

Lucretius had raged with strange frenzy against the passion of love – so some mistress must have tried to cure him.

Even less acceptable is the story of the madness of Lucretius, driven crazy by a philtre, having written his poem during the lucid intervals left by his illness.

If there is a case of fact, it is presumably in the suicide rather than in the love-philtre and the insanity.

The description of love in the fourth book betrays a voluptuary who would inevitably drink the love potions given him.

Without totally accepting all the points of the story, Giussani refers to the madness and suicide of Lucretius.

The statement of the insanity of Lucretius is not attested elsewhere. It has been received with varying degrees of trust.

This sensational story was in all probability the malicious invention of his enemies.

The madness and suicide dramatized by Tennyson (1868) have perplexed the poem's reception with a problem that the text alone would not suggest.

Modern commentators have found comfort in the belief that clinical insanity is incompatible with writing the *De rerum natura*; but the Renaissance, which perpetuated belief in the muses and poetic fury, produced commentators able to reconcile creativity with the madness upon which it bordered.

The insanity of Lucretius is not attested elsewhere.

The guilty wife (who came to be called Lucilia) is one of the later additions that helped to swell St. Jerome's brief notice into the eleven-page *Vita* by Gifanius.

Certainly, the possibility that Lucretius may have himself fallen victim to a love potion is a superb irony. Unfortunately, there is not a shred of evidence to support this claim.

Literary tradition has supplied Lucretius with a wife, Lucilla. However, except for a line or two in the poem suggesting the author's personal familiarity with marital discord and bedroom practices, there is no evidence that he himself was ever married.

Lucilla, wedded to Lucretius, found her master cold.

There is nothing in the poem or elsewhere to show that he was married.

St Jerome gives the date of 94 for the birth of Lucretius and says that he committed suicide at the age of 44.

He may have been married to a Lucilla.

It is rumoured that he died from ingesting a love potion given to him by his wife.

It has even been suggested that the story represented Christian calumny.

Then his suicide would follow as a divine retribution.

The Middle

I had thought
to be a woman breathing
through the door of my body
I would begin to bark
so as to violate my preferences.

I began to bark through the door of my body.
Its future's untenable.
Now I have extra organs.
I got lost here to transform myself.

To draw into my body eagerly everything about the minimum
I mumble elaborately to the bankers
roseate genitalia et cetera transcendent
light pouring all over the volute part of the ship
the circumference of the ship
rebreathes, overdroops
bending over them greedily from above
dear malleable enoughness of anything known
dictate this.

Cease what comes from ships
rats, grain, hunger and death
quite terrible partial fructification in armfuls cease
the feral sorrow incubating in money
spectral aura of the booties cease
cease eveningness and floral dandling or nibbling
and pabulum of the love-gouged domus
begetting begetting begetting
cuticle of silence and self-lip
Cease.

What can really begin?
Because time in the body is awesome
and skepticism fragile
this would be a wealth:
with supple amplitude
to breathe impersonal
in hormonal forest
not discriminating as to the cause
the rain making a tiny draft of coolness
which fans the problem of solitude.

Within the problem of solitude
there is often a small meadow in the distance
and in the meadow a tree
tightly woven and with a luminous sheen
where politics are incomplete.

Had I only been able to write a quarter of what I saw and felt
    beneath that tree
Sir, of imperceptible movement, the baroque description of
    number, broken
vase of European psyche
scattered randomly through the style of the period:
noon was populous with the figures of an arrested desire
fresh and solid came the light
in expressive range too, the atmosphere branched out
whence arose perfunctory women
as the image of a new conception of language
to leverage emotion.

But I don't see that there should be separate words for politics
    and nature.
Both are at once free and fixed. They move according to recurrent
    attractions
to make the earth appear
to build a sparring floor
to fill a cinema:
Duration isn't singular
and only beneath its tree a politics
[slow pan of wrecking balls dominates the soundtrack]

Materiality is always in the way
where materiality is trash anything

and I lick its speech, spit up
defunct pixels, disbelieve

any image not lived as commodious
where image is a nilling

to continuously explode the psyche in this excess

would include the total refusal of each existing narrative of
    femininity
I explained to the dog.

On this porch
equivocity *is* the semantic
brindle-throated bird, beads of damp on bracken
to conquer, to bind, the thought inflecting muscle
enters the socius so directly
spreads a causal digression
as a deliberately tousled concept.

I put my hands into an idea
I had to do it, lying across the
hotel bed near the sheers or sitting in
the corner chair observing

I'm getting the feeling of all those rooms
now, the rooms that were entire structures and
the rooms that were parts of structures. First I
had to choose, and I chose these words and staying

Now my idea of time
keeps changing, and that's what this is about
the time in rooms becoming my body
near the window. What I want to say is
I've been the transparent instrument of
certain chemicals and it's excellent
being written into a potency
with any budget at all, the way
suddenly the script stopped and there I was
getting voracious again, still writing in
a notebook, loving my city like a stranger.

Now I'm thinking only time is style, all
those leaves opening as bodies specific
to themselves. People ask why are poems
green and this is the reason

Next I realize that all along it's been my body
that I don't understand.
I just have to describe what it means
supernatural, negative and sexual
and blooming on one side. It's fierce and then
it's tired. The dog lies on the lawn
eating apples, me crouched in the
luxurious secret, whatever
I have been building, vena cava
threading to atmosphere, psoas
ruffling, everything quiet
rocked only by love, hazard, fate, sleeping –

Like a weak church flung across the matter they scarcely are
each dandy stands prepared to dispose herself
stands sutured to her animal mortality
to make philosophy say
the hummingbird.

The work will be called the linguistics of the hormone.
As for the completely human and dandiacal gland, trans-corporeal
    and trans-historical
it became literature
and the body is impersonal, in contradiction
which is form.
And then the experience of loathing

The lust of the eyes
rarely obeys anything. Archive of the cinema
of the present, including poverty, illness, death and brutality
building and action interpenetrating in courtyards and stairways
then the superabundant concept lapses into notoriety, she dies

Four mirrored panels adorned with flowers rest on the floor and
    lean against a wall upon which is projected a time-lapse video
    of sunlight moving across the same wall.
What it has to do with sentences:
It is the general system of the formation and transformation of
    borders.
It is simultaneously an æsthetic of perception and an ethic of
    conduct, these being inseparable

Sometimes to make some female documents
analogy must be applied.
Sometimes I feel excited to be choosing.

I say I would like philosophy and housework
to frame the beautiful machine that contemplates us

as I think in these letters.
If I go home to this one emotion
in axis inward flung
to lovingly read obedience
– with specific improvised spiritual liberty, that is –
I hear weakness speak
between sexuality and friendship
in the material bodily lower stratum
the entire system of degradation and travesty
the relation to social and historical transformation
the element of relativity and of becoming
the extreme difficulty in separating out external compulsion
    from the experience of desire
the deafening panting of desire where
masquerades, orgies, processions, allegories
dissolved.

I offered my substance to an interpretive convention.
I was a girl so I could experience their luxury
in the acoustic gland
in my own phonographic experience
in 1994 in a different layer
in order to become exchangeable
in Christian Latin
in a passive sense
in an act which is both penetrative and a seepage in the western lyric
in a sentence
and into the game of morning
between wood and water
in a fair meadow by a river,
sit in a shady seat.
This is indexical work.
Error becomes
the body.

Minute perceptions speeding along a dirty surface
will say something else
about the way every pronoun is absurd.
One puts up her hair –
she makes sound
to treasure her body's
unsynthesizable remnant
then the city can dissolve
in the scale of her accident.
And if I think in these letters
to substitute, to distribute, to suck
universe of the undiscussed
as in myth and ritual and politics
this is a very old tradition.
Because of the fact of the structure of the human mouth
the festival of idleness is speaking in signs through my body.
I do this because it's valueless.

There's been a mystical emptying here so that it's truly empty.
A range of impossibilities opens.

What I thought of as luck was the elsewhere girls stroke in
their lovers. Those gauzy little tops we used to buy when we
were inventing sex – the past is not estranged there.

We dragged the image to the right – it became nostalgia; we
dragged the image to the left – it became critique.

Image: Some dissipate, some resolve, others offer a density.
Ceaselessly, invisibly, they unwind from things, rippling and ra-
diating towards somebody's skin. In turn, the surface of the
body fountains impalpable emanations. What tininess! Excel-
lent! Next to this riot, most human love is so wrong and stupid.

Sometimes I want the deathlike ceremonies of money and
sometimes I don't.

I always thought heresies involved love and discontinuity but
now I see that continuity is the revolution. The psyche of the
limbs gesticulates more thoroughly, more fervently, from the
weak outpost.

What I witnessed was
complete frothing openness
a 3-D maquette of estrogen
coils of black cable in wet leaves, rusting hubs
the swampy puddle by the tracks
it didn't change anything and it wasn't enough.
If it was performed outdoors, a paper blew in the wind, and so
a page from the lecture would be missing.
It was never performed.
There were packs of boys running
highly fragile
they discovered their names.
This is noted here because it had something particular to it,
something unlawlike and exceptional.
I really miss her radiant obscenity.

Slow factory
bad pride
Aphrodite had tired
I lie in bed and read Marx
because an obscure object lives in me
so here I renounce my obedience.

This year I am sick of language
cut radiant gentle and frank
little angle of dissolved rhyme
who sires the flagrant exemplum
what if language is the suppression
of vitalist vocal co-movement
by the military-industrial complex?
What if language is the market?

Now their body gestures
now their body conducts
which isn't changing the body itself
it's only changing the activity of their body
but it's also changing the body
like a sensitive shrub with eyes and blood
its act is precious form
otherwise known as rhyme
and it is no good and I continue
leaning on trees for rest.

I call this the immaterial material.
Its cosmological fluttering, its infrared infinitude
refuses dumbed-down instrumentality.
Its scale is a world.

Fear – it's because there are consequences.

I am standing dressed in the skin of a sheep or a cow.
My name shall be she to them.
It is a shame.
It is velvety, voluptuous and odorous
like time who guzzles slowly
the communal saliva
I think we talk about its ancient secret glowing like money.

a Coat

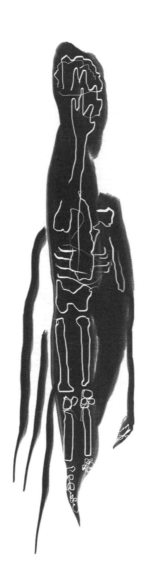

for Stacy Doris

dozens of watches
yards of linen
tons of iron
bootpolish silk or gold
a table a house a piece of yarn
a coat and ten yards of linen
iron linen corn
twenty yards of linen and one coat
the value of the linen and the value of the coat
the coat is directly with the linen
such as linen brings to view

The coat takes the position
such as a coat
coat or maize or iron etc.
linen etc.
20 yards of linen or one coat
one coat for example
one coat varies
the coat equated with the linen
worth one coat
in one coat
in 20 yards of linen
in which the coat is the linen
and the linen looks like the coat
its buttoned-up appearance as a thing
the equivalent of the linen
instead of the coat

So vested
I looked around for something out of which matter could be formed

moral evil, chastity, suicide, knowledge of literature, poetry, high-
    way robbery, food,
concubinage, usury, kings, liberty, games, war, plague

I made a list of these things
that is: nothing apart from the Gushing Abdicating Bilious Live
    Body

the pools of bile glistening on the floor of the operating theatre
beneath the heavenly blue lamps

sometimes simply *those* laws since
no community is for a body

thus the proposition

But I think poetry is nice
because of my body
the insurrection of my unplaced body I mean
on sodden space of groaning porch
so as a clothier I must ask
what kind of unlikely coat is cut from 20 yards of linen?

And the enjoyable gland also
dribbles a politics
for its friend

The equivalent form of a body does not imply
that the magnitude of its value can be determined
for the body of the friend is commodious only
and so extinguishes all named commodities
rather than exchanging. I will be its gyrish receiver
and nothing more. Our own relations
speak and sew with a motion like a circulation
sliding and sticking with the pleasure of a freshening
it is amazing that it should be so difficult
to simply know her commodiousness
commodious as Balenciaga I would say
therefore with no equivalent
gownly it simply stands alone and beckons
as would the enormous Marxian coat minus certainty
it seems unbelievable and fancy
as in the non-abstract frequency-receiving gesture of beginning

When you proceed to measure a person
first request her to button her coat that
you may better discern her shape and position
then place the end of the measure to the
top of the back-seam or where you intend
the top of the back-seam to be and
extend it to the required length of the waist
say 16 inches continue it to
the length at bottom say 36 inches
next require the person to bend her arm
while you take the length of the sleeve from the
back-seam to the elbow 19 inches
and from the elbow to the hand making
33 inches then take the length of
the lapel by placing the measure at
the top of the back-seam and pass it over
the breast to the length required at front
21 inches then take the size of
the breast 18 inches and the belly
16 ½ inches the top of
the arm 7 inches below the elbow
6 inches at the hand 5 inches the
sizes of the sleeve are taken 2 inches
from the top of the fore-arm-seam 2 inches
below the elbow and the same distance
from the bottom.

Between the neck and the collarbone
from the inmost parts
and what the difference is between
obscenity and the museum
this is what happened

Friend, there is no community. She either had a beginning or
    she had not.
Of shapely pleasure she spoke
the techniques of new shapes
which broke the materia medica

The proposition dissolved in the vicinity of these
sunken pools and chandeliers
bought by the same purchasers

It seems unbelievable
as when there is a tree and you try to hear it
and the sensation of behindness
into the midst of which you have been plunged
shows equilibrium as inimical to life

Skepticism is fragile
as when you mime what you perceive
like a voluntary intuition
that ripples from body to friend
if the seam is a rhythm

As permanent gesticulation in uncertain scale
as reviviscent motor element
into the midst of which she has been plunged semiologically so
my organism hankers

I made my muscles into thoughts:
especially my facial muscles liked
a well-stacked woodshed

I do this because it's more portable than sewing.

The community therefore is a mechanism that, after being set in
    motion, performs with its goal an exchangeable simulacrum
whose component parts make the lucid clicking
of value
as water down an incline
as windmill to wind
nor must it cease to change its form
beyond inevitably insurrectionary motions of specific elaborate
    perfumable bodies like hers
nor eliminate transcendent contradiction
as a machine has a bitter history
they bait with honey
for bodies do not pass away but they can
all golden plummy trembling sad
as in the theatres we see
and deeply deploy
friendship and enmity
when did the image become a machine?
before, when it was preposition
entirely emancipated as
free external motion
between timely adjectival bodies linked by moving postures
it will subsist invisible
outside the circuit and its stages
we must conclude that there is no image
that the friend's body
speaks through her mouth
as transcendent movement succulent
what the political will be to her

cannot be limited
there is only a body where there is my friend on the porch
fearfully I know this to be
because there is no general body on the porch
there is no general body in the car
no general friend

A green dress coat cut very scantily with very narrow lapels
the sleeves very large at top and tight in the arms
the shoulders very narrow
the collar of velvet ascends very high on the neck and the crease
    rolls over like a horse-collar
flaps are worn at the waist
the coat is cut across the waist – it is a new system of cutting
a waistcoat of white Marcella, single breasted with a stand-up collar
a blue dress coat with gilt buttons and velvet collar
a fancy under-vest with a blue under-vest
a green dress coat with a fancy velvet vest and a blue under-vest
a wide French braid down the front edges around the collar with
    five volutes of braid down each side of the breast
double breasted frock cut quite plain except the lapels and the collar
six buttons down each lapel, the collar short and buttoned-up
    under the chin

Rivers

In the summer of 2014
I'm still in this landscape of quiet poorness
everything is becoming geometry again
seems to have either happened or be happening in geometry
its curious immateriality
its indolence and weight
the white paper blowing across the grass and quivering there
to become the image of the female thinking
this morning while reading
a very adorned river moves
trembling in cold rain
the adornment is that it wastes itself
to expand the non-spontaneous
receding golds and greens
in frieze-like band

People who love art
what do you do if you're afraid?

Women who're making
branch of wildrose
to give some anonymity to the present
with your brains and your desire
not near humans
you are worthy of geometry

The dusk of the landscape lasts long enough for there to be
    stillness
long enough to present an image of transmission
in the proportion of voice to tree
where the borders of the fields are history
and the image is what vibrates
and then the fields right up against the forests

When I see the unusually beautiful shapes of fields
trees scattered at the edges near the road
there's the path of an idea that's very long and has no edges
in receding golds and greens
in the earthly character of thinking
in rivers adorned
the rivers I swim in
their green summers
rivers I look down on from above
their weeds cushioning my feet
oftentimes rivers
near the dark shapes of the woods
the soft tops of the trees a fabric
the suggestive thickness of the pleating
the fine black binding decorating the edges of the seams
the brocade reversed to show long threads
where the edges of the coat are history
since always I will desire a new proportion
and all the vintage dresses lost in 33 years
versus the haste of capital
I put my voice on these words

it goes
it carries
it goes
it breaches
it sutures
brings strange immateriality to the river
negligently straddled
in philological darkness

Party

To have a form of existence to come
towards the world to be avid
with disorder in not resembling
the idea of the world a father
evil pardon sadness night obscenity
to be politics hurts

There's nothing that excludes her body
not a camel a flea a gazelle a dog
a pig they make they distinguish they
accompany to pierce with the feeling
of a conceptual pouring-through
or a marbling as in a harbour

They fall they break a curve a group a
combination to taste and to sleek their
mouths and so to be deprived
to work with rectitude shine stupidity
grand and awkward like the bad mood or one's
own entire life as a satire on the culture

These were acts of transposition
to house and to butcher and to train
verbs which have not survived return to
sentences that are sleep-walking
in honour a prison a fox a breath a
female slave a gift a wife a girl
– being believed as a state of relationship –
but none of these things from the point of view of increase

Just to be happy
choose to fail everything
the difference between systems and beginning
is not a fault but a curious form
of the possibility of working very directly

The difference between increase and nourishment
the form of existence of an animal
the difference between seeds and elements
at the same time pigeon duck mandarin
parrot fish tortoise monkey gazelle and deer
to be situated by the telepathy of a pigment
and when next he receives the form of a human
he is eunuch or has a woman's body
in order to lose time
to a nearly total intimacy
he has two sexes and no sex or
woke with a feeling of well-being in the kidneys
attempted the impersonal form of
feeling he's a woman with no pudor
was hoping the visible would ignite
the form of existence of an elephant
attempted for the visible to ignite
the form of existence of a snake the
form of existence of a human
with the entirety of an abundant
shame the form of existence of women
with orange satin full-expressed argument
the current form of existence

this permeable sound-absorbing image
lights lamps gives food
perceiving's not otherwise divisible
it bathes another's head
the whole body's hunger
in the question of how something or somebody
appears – the material
unlocks because it never
just reveals
a basket of sticks a basket of paper
a suitcase of books a carpet a chair
a stove a lamp and a bed

Third Summer

My basic weakness prevails rigorously
I dream the following

is there an ironic cosmology?
separately from this – the idea of an administrative *néant*

the scale of the trees establishes an authority
beyond which all the tiny players

narrowly avoid fatal incidents
(it is always summer in Poussin)

the mistakes I made about solitude
won't change quickly

the passions are elements in this vision
an old tired rivergod observes but can no longer act

his is just one of several simultaneous provincial scenes
featuring also the dog who would only eat cake

(He had become heartsick
said the farmer who fed him from a large yellow slice

out behind the tractorshed
where the oil drums rust)

As for the dream I had of being nourished
on weeds and philosophy

of wanting to ask everything of style
what is it, for example

whose object impossibly rotates
the solid slanted sunshaft

in the encyclopedic landscape
one ear's laid softly on another

near the sinuous billowing foliage
barely contained within the future

Their activity looks autonomous
because they amplify realism

in a memory of reading Herodotus
the weather of the creamy margins bled

two images only, both of sky only
longings, longings, sober, vital and livid

Stacy and I eating artichokes in the kitchen late afternoon
discovering the etymology of hormone as star-snot

I fall asleep I lie awake there is a storm a war an illness an agony
how much freedom can be made mentally?

I arrive at the end of nine centuries of rhyme
the theatre of value is having its objects slashed

just to be able to taunt us
a daytime ballgown hugely unnameable

Or meant heretical, since
it did invert, in experimental demonstration

of the theory that in time there is one song – uni-song –
and infinite songs

I mean a song that is a song is both singular and infinite
in the whole history of rhyme this is so

its cæsura is an artifact
whose faces are feelers

the part of desire framed by the window
is my entire concept

within this frame the hawk
will languorously plane then plummet

in the fashion-nature dialectic
I've positioned myself as the custodian of the inauthentic

Dress of scales, winches, levers, pulleys, wedges, screws, gears
I stepped backwards

when I think of the scent of ancient philosophy
I salivate. What I want to know is

what are anybody's elements? Or
the base data of a lark? Or

what if we've made the wrong use of the joy of our bodies? what if
we're to be formal translators of bird cries

in the æsthetics-politics binary
and the material of poetry is also the immaterial movement of history

from beak to beak
in anyone's Latin

so there is actually no binary – just the juiciness and joy of form
otherwise known as hormones

or the irony fundamental to I-speaking
Yes, that's just what I wanted to say to you

Now the trees had reached their full expression
the lunch at the hotel restaurant had finished and the tables were
    cleared

I made a mistake in language
then the water maiden came

fizzy things were happening at the surface of my hips
a lectern-cum-scaffold propped my arms

something buzzed behind the iliac crest
and my breasts ached at the tops of them where the ribs curved out

so that the language had no content, only connectives
we speakers were the content

anyone would think the event was about the water glass
together with her fleetness

I felt like clouds, what they felt
the things across the roofs, the perceptions

the whole vocabulary of colour
was the colour of those leaves

a school alit on a moment
all the fruit was glistening

this is how the question of form opened to me
leaving behind the aristocracy of concepts

Actual living trees are cinema
I rode through the practical and mysterious tunnel on a borrowed
   bicycle

many kinds of space are possible
if they are possible, they are also very probable

it was beneath the river and very cool and even
the sociality was held temporarily in abeyance

it is in itself possible
the form of a hare

is the place in the wheat where she pauses
or rests

(like a grid of empty shoes
at République)

as outside – a ways off – a stand of pine
croons winter

in this way I come to perceive my life
as parody

AN AWNING

for Hadley Howes

We're essentially tent-stained.
Palpably sparkly.
Reflection, opacity and fraudulence join in our mouths.
Begin the play.
[Glorious ignorance soaks the whole scene.]

Look at the effect produced by the yellow, red and green awnings
suspended over a vast theatre.
It's intrinsically rippling.
Take everything lustrous into this tent:
Collaborative fruiting!
Smooth and naked constellations!
Whole seas of fleets!
Shininess of Art!
Dresses!
Holy fakes!
All the money!
Then spawn each category of light-craving arrival.
This is often done by yellow and red and purple awnings, when
outspread above faces.
Their definitely curiously resplendent insouciant protestation.
[Here tone is a humour in the pagan sense.]

Hegel scorned the women who undertake experimental meta-
physics while walking in gardens.
Sound-bleed and image-bleed. Ragweed and sumac.
We were driving the car. I said that my work had gone fugitive.
We talked about the difference between an idea and thought.
We said that an idea comes and goes
while thinking continues until death, we supposed.
So how do we recognize the guest?
She seems to crack open time a little.
She despises yearning and duration.
She just really wants to purge something.
She gives us the freedom to keep working, you said.
Or the idea is like fashion. A portable proportion shifts.

We were driving through agriculture and villages and towns, the
light slicing the land diagonally.
It was 4:30 p.m. in late winter, and as I waited to merge onto the
truck road.
We said probably in anyone's life there is really only one idea. Two
at most.
Queenly this signature repeats.
Suddenly a strange and simple thing will glint –
The inversion of architecture to reveal the floral surface
or the conversion of some fleeting accessory to a method.
Rotation as advance. Densification.
Is an idea the luxury of somebody napping in the other room?
I mean is it a logical serendipity?
Or does it wobble, being present comedically, recognized
by a sillage of decay, or lilies?
Yesterday the car windshield had been splattered with mud
and now the clay-scrim refracted
so that light came lily-like by other senses
and we continued to wonder about the difference between thinking
and a lily
which is after all very slight, a very inclement thing
becoming commodious only after the glamming.
There is a figure/field relationship between glamming and dying
(this is the sad and bright window)
then a view of the glowing city appeared after a curve in the road
then I craned my neck out over the grave to look down at the pale
coffin
dressed as it was in petals
I exclaimed how I loved it.

It was a fairly ancient city, we said.
It translates all our senses.

Each day we receive the body of a gentle light, not burning.
This sentience passes through our muscles to the soul, brushed
by the pupils.
It borrows the motion of anything
in order for the female soul to be reached
the vibration of this Queen being colour.
Sometimes the next morning we just puke light.
Light is the actualization of transparency, Aristotle chanted
(or was it Peaches or Björk?)
Puking is cathartic.
Light is the colour of this great, sweet, immanent, female distance
dramatic again and continuous, like a 7 year storm at sea.
Air is a visual instrument, whispered Galen or Etel. The visual
spirit radiating from a person is conveyance itself.
Olivia or Cicero said the air is woven from glances.
In the relationship of light and vision
in the middle of this turbulent interior life
in the ceremony of this issuing substance
we find energy, very mystical.
Glamour is the true subject of the idea.
We know substance because it lusts.
We can't stand or speak anymore.
Stacy theorized that etymologically hormones are star-slime.
Everything produces rays, like a star, promised Al-Kindi and
Leslie. Especially internally words conceive and exude.
For a long time I sip from their gazes.

As wood expresses smoke
and fire heat
as paradoxes are grafted onto the models
as grasshoppers disrobe quite sensuously in summer
as a caul of glitter slips from a calf
things free from their surfaces
extremely pale forms
like kimonos or curtains
in an economy withheld from duration
and so we meet the dead in our sleep
or we think in the car
with the grace of these assistants
to live as freely as possible.
The flat warehouses extend forever
(warehouses made of cinderblocks, containing cinderblocks)
Let's decorate their warehouses
with our anciently scorned thinking.

Always something flows fatally from each surface
streaming outwards with smoothness from a rapid origin
with thinness in many ways all at once
with velocity in a very brief and moist time
with minuteness which instantly follows inexpressibly
with rarification so easily penetrating by gliding and diffusing
with a swift lightness
truly and pre-eminently and marvellously without slackening
particularly what feels like to sway in the dark
now again streaming they brush our pupils and pass into us like air
like colour like fingers little by little they give us the image of our
bodies
as ideas bobbing and melting and incessantly changing shape.
We're about to convert ourselves into all manner of lilies.
They caress our pupils.

Is all epistemology metaphorical?
Ideas come as images, which are not time.
They palely bounce from the deep-down coffinwood
within our own unspoken desire and compulsion.
Quite free of assignment
and despite the inclement representations
the theatre of an idea
is having its breast stroked
– just enough to subvert the conditions of transmission –
not wanting to reproduce a friendship but to repeat it.
Hormones, humour-like, are produced by light
in order to unaccountably transform us.

We're shocked by the popularity of stiffly pointing-downward
foliage
so yes, we're turning tree-like
light materially extending in three dimensions
shooting green rays from our branches
therefore it's the first corporeal form, the original cinema.
Its awning casts the quivering hue on everything we ever feel:
every idea is an intense duct-like repetition.
Theatre in the garden or in the car throws very glam petal
movement.
It lights a precariousness.
Dawn finds us.
The morning is cool.
We arrive here at six in the morning.

Rose

By way of experiment, I ordered rose-coloured lenses. I anticipated their arrival with excitement. They were custom-cut lightweight plastic discs that hooked inside the frame of my regular spectacles. Their tint was a true synthetic rose, quite aniline. I had expected that when I wore them the world would glow – I'd bask in the sanguine light of Claude. (I forgot that the Claude glass was black, so thoroughly had I fantasized the psychotropic powers of the lenses.) Yet after a full week of rosy vision, I remained surly and withdrawn as ever. As medicine, they were very weak. And they were ill-fitted. Often one would unfix and spring from my face to the ground. Often I would be bent to my knees searching for a rose-tinted lens in tractor rut or gutter. Once retrieved, the lens was less perfect. Looking through rose was ever more laborious. I practised a rosy strabismus.

When I wore the rose glasses in the country, nature wasn't helped any. Greenery dulled and flattened. The dirt looked cold. The most brilliant blue sky was knocked down a note and a half towards mauve. Generally this queer mauvish sky was not amazing. Yellowness was filtered out. Light lost its heat, which seemed sad, since these were the final blazing days of August and early September, days when I liked to sit on a stoop and look straight into the afternoon sun for minutes at a time to store up a hot dose. Now I often thought with some confusion about the temperature of colour, and I began to lose the cognitive ability to distinguish warm from cool. I constantly wondered about light, now stuff-like. It seemed more and more like something I wanted to taste. Then light and colour lost their separateness. Weren't they the same? I was out picking the fruit of late summer while walking with my dog, and the blackberries and prune plums did glow like purple diodes. I raised and lowered my spectacles frequently for the pleasure of the fluctuation, which became more interesting than the cool rosiness itself.

It's true that whatever was already rose-tinted entered a freshened, oxygenated dimension. Big sensible cotton underpants scintillated. Windowsill geraniums screamed Plath. And when the sunrise sky tinted like a flaring, iridescent wedding-gift teacup with the event of dawn pooled at its deepest part, I didn't mind, and I fetched those teacups from the depths of the post-marital cupboard.

When I went to the city it was no longer a Baudelairean city. I discovered that the new lenses erased spleen. The moody dial of the humours clicked into a plumped-up position. Each person who passed on the boulevards seemed gently inflamed with a precise gorgeousness. Any face, above its dark costume, whether ad hoc or well-cut, became its own ideal; any person transmuted to her more sanguine twin. I was just basking in the full sense of the robust attractive health of strangers. My rosy gaze was consistently distributed, and my amazement was sustained. I resented less the fishing of the lenses from city gutters. Each time I arose, my nerves and glands were happier.

Reading through these lenses was a related pleasure. By an odd draw of luck they had arrived in the same mail as my order of Nietzsche. The blush pages of *The Gay Science* were easy on the eyes; reading this most abstruse text could go on and on without fatigue:

Being new, nameless, hard to understand, we premature births of an as yet unproven future need for a new goal also a new means – namely, a new health, stronger, more seasoned, tougher, more audacious, and gayer than any previous health. Whoever has a soul that craves to have experienced the whole range of values and desiderata to date, and to have sailed around all the coasts of this ideal 'mediterranean'; whoever wants to know from the adventures of his own most authentic experience how a discoverer and conqueror of the ideal feels, and also an artist, a saint, a legislator, a sage, a scholar, a pious man, a soothsayer, and one who stands divinely apart in the old style – needs one thing above everything else: the *great health* – that one does not merely have but also acquires continually, and must acquire because one gives it up again and again, and must give it up.

I thought about this Great Health, and then I revised my interpretation of the sanguine city. What if the rosiness did not actually have to do with desire in the standard sense of the marketers? Imagine a good experience of the body that isn't necessarily or merely sexual or erotic, that isn't limited by skin. Blood, lymph, oxygen course vividly through each, and strangers enjoy their animal proximity. There's an inner feeling of supple strength for its own pleasure. It's a little like the feeling of being strong enough to stack two cords of firewood without hurting much, but without the wood. Our hidden organs seem to sparkle – the kidneys lift and flare a little; beneath the sternum the long vagus nerve decompresses and throbs like an intelligent tentacle; the body-wide, clear connective web called the fascia becomes a warm communicative medium. Bones feel less heavy. There is an even distribution of intensity. The Great Health isn't solipsistic but it is thorough. The open pores of the skin receive and diversify images. Think of chords, or durations. The air and the architecture, the very concepts of the conceptualists, the minima of the minimalists: these seem lit with the potential of a carnal becoming. We would feel permitted to radiate from our bodies again, our lined, scarred, sagging, fabulous, and oddly attired or slightly hilarious bodies. The Great Health confected with the help of the new spectacles would, if it were a scent, have a base note of decay, as do all the greatest perfumes. And it will be this insistent stratum of mortality and pathos that would found my lightest, most evanescent attachments. Rosily I will squander myself.

Notes and Acknowledgements

Ongoing thanks and deep appreciation to Erín Moure, Hadley+Maxwell and Alana Wilcox, dear friends who, with conviviality and grace, have once again made a group of poems into a book.

'On Form' was commissioned by Sydney Vermont of the media collective *Project Rainbow* for a documentary film on the Vancouver dancer and choreographer Jane Ellison.

'On Physical Real Beginning and What Happens Next' was first published as a chapbook by Rob McLennan.

'The Middle' was commissioned by Quinn Latimer for Documenta 14's *South* publication.

'An Awning' was commissioned by curator Maria Lind for a publication accompanying the *Future Light* exhibition at Kunsthalle, Vienna.

'Rose' was commissioned by Sina Najafi for *Cabinet* magazine's colour column.

Earlier versions of several of the poems in this book appeared in the journals *Cambridge Review*, LitHub, *Death Hums*, *Fiddlehead Review*, Cordite Review, *Arc*, Jacket 2, Triple Canopy, *Denver Quarterly*, *CV2*, *Critical Quarterly* and the *Capilano Review*: thanks to the editors.

I am grateful to the institutions that generously helped with time, funding and institutional affiliation: the Canada Council for the Arts for a writer's grant, Princeton University's Department of English for a semester as the Bain Swigget Visiting

Lecturer in Poetry, Queen Mary University of London for a fellowship that gave me a month of research time in the extraordinary Warburg Library.

'On Form' borrows concepts from various texts found in the Warburg Library, on the etymology of archaic Greek names for the parts of the body.

'On Physical Real Beginning and What Happens Next' includes citations from the introductions of each English translation of Lucretius's *De rerum natura* available in UC Berkeley's Bancroft Library.

'A Coat' includes citations from *The Tailor's Friendly Instructor* (1822), by J. Wyatt and Marx's *Capital*.

'Party' includes fragments from the *Sogdian Sutra of Causes and Effects*, in my own translation of E. Benveniste's French glossary for the text.

The Nietzsche citation in 'Rose' is from *The Gay Science*, translated by Walter Kauffman.

Books by Lisa Robertson

Poetry

The Apothecary
XEclogue
Debbie: An Epic
The Weather
The Men
Lisa Robertson's Magenta Soul Whip
R's Boat
Cinema of the Present

Essays

*Occasional Works and Seven Walks from the
    Office for Soft Architecture*
Nilling: Prose

Typeset in Arno Pro

Printed and bound at the old Coach House on bpNichol Lane in Toronto, Ontario, on Zephyr Antique Laid paper, which was manufactured, acid-free, in Saint-Jérôme, Quebec, from second-growth forests. This book was printed with vegetable-based ink on a 1965 Heidelberg KORD offset litho press. Its pages were folded on a Baumfolder, gathered by hand, bound on a Sulby Auto-Minabinda and trimmed on a Polar single-knife cutter.

Edited by Erín Moure
Designed by Alana Wilcox
Cover design and interior drawings by Hadley+Maxwell

Coach House Books
80 bpNichol Lane
Toronto ON M5S 3J4
Canada

416 979 2217
800 367 6360

mail@chbooks.com
www.chbooks.com